The Funny Thing about
Fatherhood

The Funny Thing about
Fatherhood

Bonnie Louise Kuchler

WILLOW CREEK PRESS®

Published by Willow Creek Press, Inc.
P.O. Box 147, Minocqua, Wisconsin 54548

Photo Credits:
p2 © Shinji Kusano/Nature Production/Minden Pictures; p5 © Michael Quinton/Minden Pictures;
p6 © Tier Images/age fotostock; p9 © D. Parer & E. Parer-Cook/Auscape/Minden Pictures; p10 © Ronald Wittek/age fotostock;
p13 © Robert Harding Images/Masterfile; p14 © Cyril Ruoso/JH Editorial/Minden Pictures;
p17 © Michael Quinton/Minden Pictures; p18 © Anup Shah/NPL/Minden Pictures;
p21 © David Curl/npl/Minden Pictures; p22 © R. Linke/age fotostock; p25 © F. Lukasseck/Masterfile;
p26 © Carol Walker/NPL/Minden Pictures; p29 © Bernard Castelein/NPL/Minden Pictures;
p30 © Wave Royalty Free/age fotostock; p33 © Mitsuaki Iwago/Minden Pictures; p34 © KITCHINHURST/age fotostock;
p37 © Konrad Wothe/Minden Pictures; p38 © Jan Vermeer/ Foto Natura/Minden Pictures; p41 © J&C Sohns/age fotostock;
p42 © W. Layer/age fotostock; p45 © Mark Raycroft/Minden Pictures; p46 © White Fox/age fotostock;
p49 © Patricio Robles Gil/NPL/Minden Pictures; p50 © Anup Shah/NPL/Minden Pictures; p53 © George Sanker;
p54 © ARCOP/Wegner/age fotostock; p57 © Suzi Eszterhas/Minden Pictures; p58 © Juniors Bildarchiv/age fotostock;
p61 © George Sanker; © p62 Cyril Ruoso/JH Editorial/Minden Pictures; p65 © FLPA/Paul Sawer/age fotostock;
p66 © Anup Shah/NPL/Minden Pictures; p69 © ZSSD/Minden Pictures;
p70 © Yva Momatiuk & John Eastcott/Minden Pictures; p73 © A. Held/age fotostock;
p74 © Andrew McConnell/age fotostock; p77 © Edwin Neeb/age fotostock; p78 © Fotofeeling/age fotostock;
p81 © Mike & Lisa Husar/Team Husar; p82 © UpperCut Images/Masterfile; p85 © Juan Carlos Munoz/NPL/Minden Pictures;
p86 © Anup Shah/NPL/Minden Pictures; p89 © R. Kaufung/age fotostock; p90 © Ingo Arndt/Minden Pictures;
p93 © Sumio Harada/Minden Pictures; p94 © Corbis/age fotostock; p96 © Juniors Bildarchiv/age fotostock

Design: Donnie Rubo
Printed in China

With Oscar-worthy sound effects, boys pit their action figures

one against another, dreaming of battles and heroes.

But how often do they give G. I. Joe a bottle?

Fatherhood brings epic change.

Your disposable income buys disposable diapers.

The song stuck in your head isn't about being born wild;

it's about visually impaired mice.

You don't know the top speed of your four-door car,

but you do know it scored big on passenger safety.

You actually say words like "blankie" and "boo-boo."

And when the word "Da-da" comes from your

child's lips for the first time, it hits you.

Whether you ever dreamed of it or not,

a father is what you were meant to be.

*A man travels the world over
in search of what he needs,
and returns home to find it.*

—GEORGE A. MOORE (1852-1933)
Irish novelist, poet, and writer

Fathers... are not born.
Men grow into fathers.

—DAVID M. GOTTESMAN, M. D.

Except that right side up is best,
there is not much to learn about holding a baby.
There are 152 distinctly different
ways of holding a baby—
and all are right.

—HEYWOOD BROUN (1888-1939)
US journalist and sportswriter

Spread the diaper in the position of
the diamond with you at bat.
Then, fold second base down to home and
set the baby on the pitcher's mound.
Put first base and third together, bring up
home plate and pin the three together.
Of course, in case of rain, you gotta call
the game and start all over again.

—JIMMY PIERSALL (B. 1929)
former Major League Baseball center fielder

Man, if I can get a burp
out of that little thing,
I feel such a sense of
accomplishment.

—BRAD PITT (1963)
US actor on *Today Show* as quoted by
People magazine, July 2006

A man prides himself on his strength—
but when his child is born he discovers
that strength is not enough,
and that he must learn gentleness.

—PAM BROWN (B. 1948)
Australian poet

*Life is a flame that is always burning itself out,
but it catches fire again every time a child is born.*

—GEORGE BERNARD SHAW (1856-1950)
Irish playwright and novelist

He has never lost his footing
with me, not in the goofy,
tumbledown way he surrendered
on first sight to his baby girl.

—KAREN MAEZEN MILLER
US author and zen teacher

I remember the very first time I held
my son in my arms as a newborn.
Everything else in the universe melted away.
There was just a father, a son, and the
distant sound of my wife saying,
"If you ever come near me again,
I'll drop you with a deer rifle."

*Parenthood:
That state of being better
chaperoned than you
were before marriage.*

—MARCELENE COX
US columnist and humorist

A baby first laughs at
the age of four weeks.
By that time their eyes
focus well enough to
see you clearly.

—DR. JONATHAN AGNEW

Children are angels whose wings decrease as their legs increase.

—FRENCH PROVERB

*A two-year-old is kind of
like having a blender, but
you don't have a top for it.*

—JERRY SEINFELD (B. 1954)
US comedian and actor

Even when freshly washed and relieved of all obvious confections, children tend to be sticky.

—FRAN LEBOWITZ (B. 1950)
US author

*Happy is the father
whose child finds
his attempts to
amuse it, amusing!*

—ROBERT WILSON LYND (1879-1949)
Irish writer and essayist

Before... I merely strode through the world like a man. Now I crawl, hunker, scramble, hop on one foot, often see the world from my hands and knees.

—HUGH O'NEILL
US writer

A man never stands as tall as when he kneels to help a child.

—KNIGHTS OF PYTHAGORAS
Masonic youth organization

My father used to play with my brother and me in the yard. Mother would come out and say, "You're tearing up the grass." "We're not raising grass," Dad would reply. "We're raising boys."

—HARMON KILLEBREW (B. 1936)
Former major league baseball player and broadcaster

There's something like a line of gold thread running through a man's words when he talks to his daughter, and gradually over the years it gets to be long enough for you to pick up in your hands and weave into a cloth that feels like love itself.

—JOHN GREGORY BROWN (B. 1960)
US novelist

Our father...
held his love up over us like an
umbrella and kept off the trouble.

—MARY LAVIN (1912-1996)
Irish writer and novelist

I always looked up to my father when I was young, but... I did a good job of hiding it.

—GREGORY E. LANG
US author and photographer

Raising kids is part joy
and part guerilla warfare.

—ED ASNER (B. 1929)
US actor

*Universal peace sounds ridiculous
to the head of an average family.*

—KIN HUBBARD (1868-1930)
US cartoonist, journalist, and humorist

I've learned that as a parent, when you have sex your body emits a hormone that drifts down the hall into your child's room and makes them want a drink of water.

—JEFF FOXWORTHY (B. 1958)
US comedian and author

Parents are the bones upon which children sharpen their teeth.

—PETER USTINOV (1921-2004)
English actor, writer, and dramatist

The important thing, I learned from my father, was to find your own bone and sink your teeth in it.

—WILLIAM PLUMMER
US author

The best advice my father gave me was,
"If you stop punching her, she'll let go of your hair."

—TERRY FIRTH

Having a family is like having a bowling alley installed in your brain.

—ALAN BLEASDALE (B. 1946)
English television dramatist

Always end the name of your child with a vowel, so that when you yell the name will carry.

—BILL COSBY (B. 1937)
US actor and comedian

For children, is there any happiness which is not also noise?

—FREDERICK WILLIAM FABER (1814-1863)
British hymn writer and theologian

Anyone who thinks the art of conversation is dead ought to tell a child to go to bed.

—ROBERT GALLAGHER (B. 1969)
British editorial photographer

Dad, you never listen. Do you just hear what you want to hear? Oh, why thank you, son. I HAVE been working out.

—MATT AND VICTOR PELLET
from *In-Laws* TV series

In an instant, Dad trumps Spiderman,
Batman, Superman, and the Hulk
when he vanquishes the monster under the bed.

—BONNIE LOUISE KUCHLER

*Father is a giant
from whose shoulders
you can see forever.*

—PERRY GARFINKEL
US author

Once you become a father, you stop being
the picture and become the frame.

—DANIEL LANG

*I did what any dad would do
when a kid says he's got a dream.
I went out there and helped him chase it.*

—DANTE BICHETTE, JR. (B. 1992)
US baseball player

*What we become
depends on what our fathers
teach us at odd moments,
when they aren't trying to teach us.*

—UMBERTO ECO (B. 1932)
Italian novelist and philosopher

Mother Nature is providential. She gives us twelve years to develop a love for our children before turning them into teenagers.

—WILLIAM GALVIN

Imagination is something that sits up with Dad and Mom the first time their teenager stays out late.

—LANE OLINGHOUSE
US writer

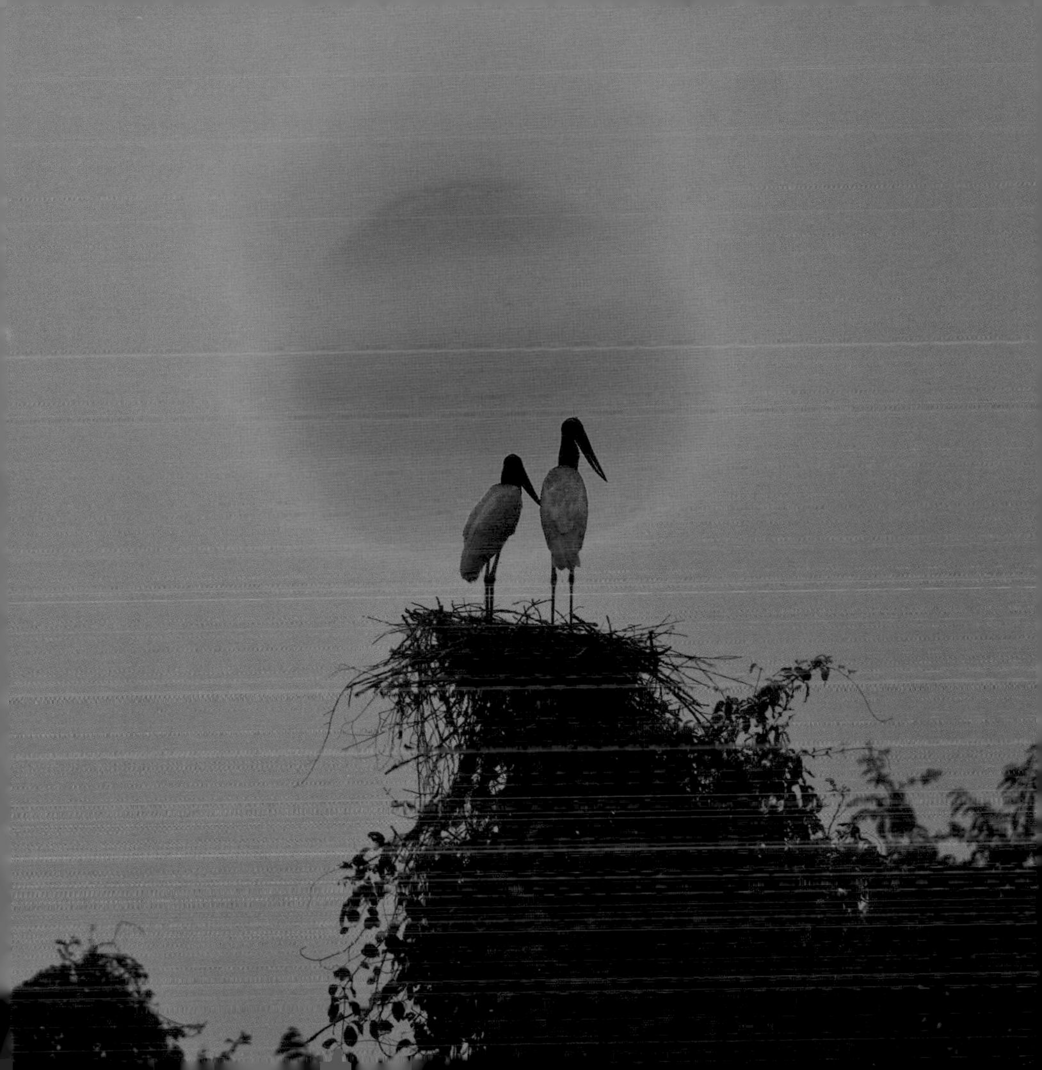

A father... is measured by
how he parents his children.
What he gives them,
what he keeps away from them,
the lessons he teaches,
and the lessons he allows
them to learn on their own.

—LISA ROGERS

A father is first a curiosity,
then an amusement-park ride,
then a referee, and finally, a bank.

—ESQUIRE MAGAZINE

The toughest part
of parenting is
never knowing if you're
doing the right thing.

—D. L. STEWART
US columnist

It's a wonderful feeling when your father becomes not a god but a man to you— when he comes down from the mountain and you see he's this man with weaknesses. And you love him as a whole being, not as a figurehead.

—ROBIN WILLIAMS (B. 1951)
US actor and comedian

*All the feeling which my father
could not put into words
was in his hand.*

—FREYA STARK (1893-1993)
British explorer and travel writer